An Introduction to ESOPs

13th Edition

Scott S. Rodrick

The National Center for Employee Ownership
Oakland, California

This publication is designed to provide accurate and authoritative information in regard to the subject matter covered. It is sold with the understanding that the publisher is not engaged in rendering legal, accounting, or other professional services. If legal advice or other expert assistance is required, the services of a competent professional person should be sought.

This publication is a concise, general overview of how ESOPs work. As such, it frequently omits special exceptions or circumstances, as well as much detail. There are many resources, including National Center for Employee Owner-ship (NCEO) publications and the informational resources available to NCEO members, that can help you explore this area further. If you do decide to proceed with considering an ESOP, you must obtain the advice of competent professionals who are experienced in the field. The NCEO maintains a search-able database of employee ownership consultants (the Referral Service) that is available online for its members at no cost.

A detailed technical review of this edition was provided by attorney Kevin Long of Chang, Ruthenberg & Long. Appraiser Kathryn F. Aschwald of Columbia Financial Advisors reviewed the chapter on valuation when it was originally written. The author thanks them for their generous assistance.

An Introduction to ESOPs, 13th ed.
Scott S. Rodrick

The National Center for Employee Ownership
1736 Franklin Street, 8th Floor
Oakland, CA 94612
(510) 208-1300
(510) 272-9510 (fax)
Web: www.nceo.org

ISBN: 978-1-932924-97-8

Contents

Introduction

In the U.S. today, more than 10 million employees in almost 11,000 companies own stock in their companies through employee stock ownership plans (ESOPs). An ESOP is a company-funded retirement plan, very similar to a profit-sharing plan, that holds company stock in accounts for the participants. Both public and private companies can set up ESOPs. ESOPs are used for a variety of reasons, including to buy out existing owners, borrow money to acquire new assets, or provide a reward system that fits today's participative management styles. These and other applications receive substantial tax benefits.

This book provides a review of how ESOPs work. It is written not as a "sales" piece but as a source of objective information for readers who are deciding whether to implement an ESOP. It also serves as a concise ESOP reference for nonspecialists.

CHAPTER 1

What Is an ESOP?

ESOPs defined. An ESOP is a qualified, defined contribution employee benefit plan that invests primarily in the stock of the employer company. ESOPs are "qualified" (i.e., tax-qualified) in that in return for meeting certain rules designed to protect the interests of plan participants, ESOP sponsors receive various tax benefits. ESOPs are "defined contribution plans." The employer makes yearly discretionary contributions that accumulate to produce a benefit that is not defined in advance. In contrast, under defined *benefit* plans (like traditional pension plans), employees are guaranteed a specified benefit funded by the company through required contributions.

Technically, an ESOP is simply a variation of a stock bonus plan or combination stock bonus/money purchase pension plan that is designed to invest primarily in employer stock. (Under a stock bonus plan, the employer pays out an employee benefit in the form of company stock. Money purchase pension plans are retirement-oriented plans that commit the company to a minimum annual contribution.) An ESOP is the only type of qualified employee benefit plan that can also borrow money from or on the credit of the employer, provided the ESOP uses the money to buy employer stock.

How ESOPs work. To set up an ESOP, a company creates an employee stock ownership trust (ESOT) (also referred to as the ESOP trust) and funds it by one or a combination of the following methods: contributing company shares; contributing cash to buy company shares; or having the plan borrow money to buy shares and then making payments to the ESOP trust to repay the loan.

Note that company contributions, not the employee-participants themselves, fund the plan. While in some cases there may be changes in other compensation when an ESOP is set up, employees only rarely buy stock directly for their ESOP accounts.

The ESOP may acquire treasury shares, newly issued shares, or shares of existing shareholders. Employees do not directly buy or hold shares through the plan. Instead, the plan trustee buys, holds, and sells the shares in the trust's name for the benefit of the employees. References in this book to stock held by the ESOP are thus to stock held by the ESOP trust. The ESOP trust may own any percentage of the company's stock. In recent years, the average percentage of shares owned by an ESOP has increased, and the typical ESOP now owns most of the sponsoring company's shares.

Normally, all full-time employees aged 21 and older participate. The plan's shares are allocated to individual participant accounts, subject to vesting requirements. Participants normally receive the stock, or cash equal in value to the stock, after they leave the company.

Uses of ESOPs. ESOPs are used for many purposes, including to:

- Use tax-deductible corporate earnings to buy shares from owners of closely held companies who wish to sell while deferring taxation on capital gains from the sale.
- Create a market for inside or outside shareholders in closely held companies.
- Allow shareholders with management responsibilities in closely held companies to sell gradually and ease out of the business over a period of years.
- Finance corporate acquisitions through the loan that buys stock for a leveraged ESOP.
- Enhance corporate performance and job satisfaction by creating a corporate "ownership" culture.
- Reward employees with a benefit tied to corporate performance while affording the company substantial tax benefits.

ESOP tax incentives. Employees participating in an ESOP are not taxed on stock allocated to their accounts until they receive distributions. Additionally, ESOPs have five significant tax advantages for corporations, employees, and selling shareholders:

- The employer can, within limits, deduct contributions to the ESOP, including both principal and interest on loans the ESOP uses to buy company stock. Companies can contribute their own shares to the ESOP and take a tax deduction for them.

- The employer, if a C corporation, generally can deduct reasonable cash dividends paid on ESOP-held stock and used to repay an ESOP loan, passed through to participants, or reinvested in company stock at the direction of participants. This is the only form of tax-deductible dividend. Only ESOP companies can take a tax deduction for their dividends.

- The owner of a closely held C corporation can defer taxation on his or her capital gains from the sale of company stock to the ESOP by reinvesting the sale proceeds in stocks, bonds, or other securities of U.S. operating companies, provided the ESOP owns 30% or more of the company's shares after the sale.

- S corporation ESOPs are not taxed on their share of corporate income. Furthermore, an ESOP's share of S corporation shareholder distributions (i.e., dividends) is retained by the ESOP and may be used to repay an ESOP loan, fund ESOP benefits, or pay ESOP administration expenses.

- Employees participating in an ESOP are not taxed on the stock allocated to their accounts until they receive a distribution (generally upon retirement, death, disability, or termination of employment).

Non-tax advantages.   Aside from the above tax incentives, ESOPs have other powerful advantages for companies.

Unlike other qualified retirement plans, ESOPs can borrow money on employer credit to acquire company stock, thus providing a market (funded with pretax dollars) for shareholders in closely held companies who want to sell.

Funds borrowed by an ESOP also can be used to repurchase shares with pretax dollars in public companies, although sellers may not defer capital gains from the sale, or to buy newly issued or treasury shares in any company. Proceeds from a sale of the company's stock to its ESOP can be used for purchasing new equipment, buying another business, refinancing debt, or any other business purpose. The company funds the ESOP's repayment of the loan with pretax dollars.

ESOP contributions also can be used to match employee 401(k) contributions, including under a safe harbor matching formula, encouraging greater participation in a 401(k) plan and making it easier to meet anti-discrimination testing requirements.

Finally, research shows that when an ESOP is combined with programs that provide opportunities for employees to share ideas and information about their work, it can result in higher productivity, corporate growth, and employee satisfaction and retention.

Advantages for employees who participate. When an ESOP is implemented, participating employees now have an additional benefit, one that is not taxed until they receive distributions (which for the most part is only after they leave the company)—and not even then if it is rolled over into an IRA or a successor plan in another company. Owning stock through the ESOP allows participants to share in the growth of their company, just as the company's original owners have.

An ESOP account can be a valuable component in a worker's retirement plan. Like any undiversified investment, however, it should be seen by employees as part of a larger retirement planning process.

The origins and present extent of ESOPs. The ESOP concept was developed in the 1950s by lawyer and investment banker Louis Kelso, who believed the capitalist system would be stronger if all workers, not just a few shareholders, could share in owning capital-producing assets. However, few companies took up Kelso's ideas, because an ESOP's authority to borrow money to buy stock for participants was based on IRS rulings and had no clear statutory authorization.

In 1973, Kelso persuaded Senator Russell Long, chairman of the tax-writing Senate Finance Committee, that tax benefits for ESOPs should be permitted and encouraged under employee benefit law. Soon, federal legislation promoting ESOPs appeared. Most importantly, the Employee Retirement Income Security Act of 1974 (ERISA), which governs employee benefit plans, established a statutory framework for ESOPs. In the following years, the number of ESOPs expanded dramatically now that sharing ownership was in the economic self-interest of company owners. From time to time since then, Congress has modified the laws governing ESOPs, most notably in the Tax Reform Acts of 1984 and 1986, the Small Business Job Protection Act of 1996, the Taxpayer Relief Act of 1997, the Economic Growth and Tax Relief Reconciliation Act of 2001 (EGTRRA), the American Jobs Creation Act of 2004, and the Pension Protection Act of 2006.

There are now approximately 11,000 ESOPs and similar stock bonus plans covering around 10.3 million employees—almost 10% of the non-governmental U.S. workforce. Although some ESOPs are found in publicly traded companies, most (about 97%) are in closely held companies. ESOPs are usually set up in healthy companies, although a handful have been used to save distressed companies. Most ESOPs are set up in companies that have at least 20 employees, due to the cost of setup and administration. ESOPs are found in companies ranging from family-owned machine shops to public companies like Proctor & Gamble.

ESOPs outside the U.S. The ESOP described here is a product of U.S. law and usually is for U.S. employees only. It is possible to extend a U.S. company's ESOP to employees in other countries, but foreign country tax, labor, securities, and currency exchange rules usually make this impractical.

ESOP companies with overseas employees can provide alternative forms of equity compensation—such as stock options, phantom stock, or restricted stock—that give employees parallel benefits but are less cumbersome and costly to set up and administer. Note: Various countries aside from the U.S. have plans called ESOPs, but they often have little or nothing to do with the U.S. ESOP; for example, in India, an "ESOP" is an employee stock option plan.

CHAPTER 2

Types of ESOPs and Their Financing

ESOPs belong to a broad category of employee benefit plans known as defined contribution plans. Other examples of defined contribution plans are 401(k) plans and profit-sharing plans. Like a small private bank, a defined contribution plan maintains a separate personal account for each participating employee. An ESOP may be funded either with a loan (a "leveraged ESOP") or with discretionary contributions (a "nonleveraged ESOP"). Additionally, ESOPs may be combined with or converted from other employee benefit plans.

Nonleveraged ESOPs. With a nonleveraged ESOP, the sponsoring employer contributes newly issued or treasury stock and/or cash to buy stock from existing owners or the company (see diagram below). Contributions generally may equal up to 25% of covered payroll, which is the combined payroll of all employees eligible for participation. Employer contributions to other defined contribution plans are included in the same 25% limit and may reduce the amount the company can contribute to the ESOP.

A Nonleveraged ESOP

1. Company contributes cash and/or stock to ESOP. 2. If cash was contributed, ESOP buys stock from shareholders and/or company. 3. Employees receive vested account balances (in stock and/or cash) when they retire or otherwise leave the company.

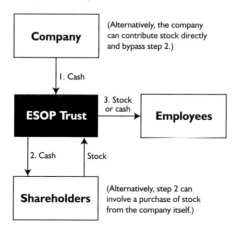

Leveraged ESOPs. A leveraged ESOP borrows money on the credit of
the employer or other related parties to buy company stock. It is the only
qualified employee benefit plan that can do so. A loan from an outside
lender can be directly to the ESOP itself, or it can be to the employer,
which then relends the money to the ESOP in a "back-to-back" loan.
Lenders generally prefer lending to the employer due to the employer's
assets and ability to secure the financing. The loan from the company to
the ESOP does not have to be on the same terms, provided its terms are
sufficiently fair to the ESOP to be the equivalent of an "arm's length"
transaction. An extension of the loan term (a longer term for the compa-
ny-to-ESOP loan than for the lender-to-company loan, e.g., to avoid violating the annual contribution limits) must meet fiduciary standards for
being primarily for the benefit of plan participants. Additional collateral
takes many forms, including personal guarantees of selling shareholders
and/or a pledge of their proceeds from the sale to the ESOP.

The ESOP loan can be used for any business purpose, such as buying
stock from existing shareholders or creating new capital by purchasing newly issued shares from the company, which can also refinance company debt.

The shares purchased by the ESOP with the loan are first placed in
a "suspense account." Then, as the loan is repaid, the shares are gradually released and allocated to participants' accounts. The percentage of
shares released each year either (1) equals the percentage of the loan
principal that is repaid for the year or (2) is based on payments of both
principal and interest for the year.

In C corporations, the contribution limit for leveraged ESOPs is generally 25% of covered payroll for contributions used to pay principal on
the ESOP loan that year. Contributions to pay interest on the ESOP loan
are not counted in the 25% limit. The law appears to allow a C corporation to separately contribute up to another 25% of covered payroll to
(1) a nonleveraged component of the ESOP itself (i.e., payments to the
ESOP that are not used to pay either principal or interest on an ESOP
loan) and/or (2) other defined contribution plans, for a total of up to 50%
of payroll plus interest payments.

The diagrams on the next page illustrate a leveraged ESOP, first with
a direct loan to the company and then with a back-to-back loan arrangement in which the company borrows money and relends it to the ESOP.

A Leveraged ESOP (Direct Loan)

1. ESOP borrows money with company guarantee. 2. ESOP buys stock from share-holders (and/or the company) and holds in suspense account. 3. Company makes yearly contributions to ESOP (3a), which in turn repays loan (3b). As ESOP repays loan, shares are released from suspense account into individual employee accounts. 4. Employees receive vested account balances (in stock and/or cash) when they retire or otherwise leave the company.

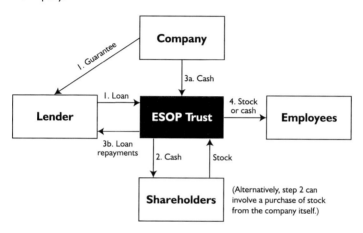

A Leveraged ESOP (Back-to-Back Loan)

1. Company borrows money. 2. ESOP borrows money from company. 3. ESOP buys stock from shareholders (and/or the company) and holds in suspense account. 4. Company makes yearly contributions to ESOP (4a), which in turn repays loan from company (4b). As ESOP repays loan, shares are released from suspense account into individual employee accounts. 5. Company in turn repays original lender. 6. Employees receive vested account balances (in stock and/or cash) when they retire or otherwise leave the company.

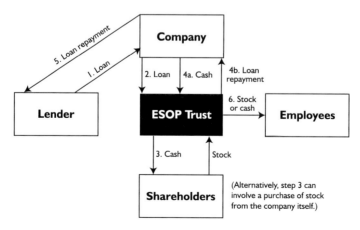

For S corporations, the contribution limit is also 25% of covered payroll. Unlike the case with C corporations, however, contributions to pay interest on the loan are included in this limit, and there are no separate 25% limits for leveraged and nonleveraged components of the ESOP, so all contributions to the ESOP (except for interest payments) and other defined contribution plans must fit within a single 25% limit.

Chapter 7, "Contribution and Allocation Limits," discusses in more detail the effect of contributions to other tax-qualified retirement plans and the potential of a C corporation to contribute a total of 50% of payroll.

Seller financing. As an alternative to bank financing, selling shareholders may wish to finance the ESOP transaction themselves. In this case, the seller(s) would receive a note from the company or the ESOP as payment for the shares. Seller financing has become more common in recent years because of the reduced availability of bank credit and because seller notes require less time, processing, and cost than bank loans and provide a reasonable rate of interest to the seller (one that reflects the level of risk involved). Because banks and other outside lenders often require a seller to back up the loan, many sellers decide that if they are taking the risk anyway, they might as well get the investment return on the loan while still selling their capital asset at a fair price.

It is preferable for the company, not the ESOP, to provide the note; for example, ERISA limits the terms the ESOP may offer when it borrows money to buy stock. Also, if the ESOP issues the note, the company must fund the payments through contributions to the ESOP, or dividends or distributions on ESOP-held stock, which can unnecessarily complicate matters for the company.

Apart from the question of whether the ESOP or the company provides the note, there are several different ways to structure a seller-financed transaction. For example, the company can borrow money for a single day from a bank, whereupon the following steps immediately happen: the company loans the money to the ESOP, the deal closes and the ESOP pays cash for the seller's stock, the seller loans that money back to the company, the company repays the bank, and the company provides a note to the seller to repay the loan.

As discussed in the next chapter, a seller to a C corporation ESOP can defer capital gains taxes under certain circumstances, but only if the gains are reinvested in qualified replacement property (QRP) within 12 months after the ESOP transaction. This presents a problem if the seller self-finances and receives installments over a period of years on a note; most of the money will be received long after it could be reinvested to avoid capital gains taxes. A solution to this is to borrow the money to reinvest in QRP, usually floating-rate notes, before the reinvestment deadline passes 12 months after the transaction. Here, the QRP serves as collateral for the loan that supplies the funds to purchase it, and the seller can use the installment payments from the ESOP and/or income from the QRP to pay down the loan.

ESOPs combined with other plans. An ESOP, leveraged or not, can be combined with another benefit plan. This provides some security through diversification if the company goes bankrupt, at which point company stock held by the ESOP may become virtually worthless. One popular combination is using leveraged ESOP contributions to fund the company match in a 401(k) plan. Of course, ESOPs can also exist side by side with 401(k) or other benefit plans without being combined with them.

Converting other plans to ESOPs. Any qualified plan may be converted to or replaced with an ESOP. An existing defined *contribution* plan, such as a profit-sharing plan, can be converted into an ESOP without terminating it. However, any conversion of a plan that involves using the old plan's assets to acquire company stock involves substantial fiduciary risk that must be carefully considered. Shifting more than 25% or so of a diversified plan's assets into an ESOP can raise fiduciary questions (see chapter 10) because those assets will now be exposed to more risk since an ESOP inherently has little or even no diversification. ESOP conversions from other types of plans may involve employee elections to transfer their account balances to an ESOP or to invest their non-ESOP accounts in ESOP shares. This may reduce fiduciary risk if properly structured; however, complex federal and state securities laws must be followed carefully.

If a company replaces an existing defined *benefit* plan (i.e., a standard pension plan with a fixed schedule of benefits) with an ESOP, the old plan is terminated, and the employees become fully vested in and have the right to receive distributions from it. Only the funds left over after paying out employees can be used to fund the ESOP. There are substantial tax costs for conversions of defined benefit plans.

CHAPTER 3

ESOP Tax Incentives

Congress has enacted tax incentives for ESOPs that provide advantages for not only the sponsoring company but also the employees, the lender to an ESOP, and selling shareholders in closely held companies. Most states have laws that automatically track these provisions, thus magnifying the tax incentives.

Deductibility of ESOP contributions. Employer contributions to the ESOP generally are tax-deductible up to a limit of 25% of covered payroll (this limit also includes employer contributions to other defined contribution plans). For a C corporation with a leveraged ESOP, the 25% limit does not include contributions to pay interest on the loan.[1] The law appears to allow a C corporation to also contribute up to an additional 25% that is not used for payments on an ESOP loan (see chapter 7).

The deduction limits for an S corporation ESOP are the same as for a nonleveraged C corporation ESOP. However, even if the S corporation ESOP is leveraged, the company is not entitled to exclude the loan's interest expense from the 25% limit. In a C corporation, the company takes the deductions and reduces its taxes. In an S corporation, the deduction reduces the taxable income that is reported on the tax returns of any non-ESOP shareholders, who then benefit from the deduction.

Deductibility of dividends paid on ESOP-held stock. C corporations can deduct dividends paid on ESOP-held stock in three ways. First, dividends may be paid in cash to ESOP participants, either directly or as payments to the ESOP that are distributed to participants within 90 days after the close of the plan year. Second, dividends may be applied to a leveraged ESOP's loan payments. (However, only dividends paid on the shares purchased with the loan may be used to make payments on the

---

1. If not more than one-third of the contributions are allocated to the accounts of highly compensated employees, these interest payments are also excluded from the per-employee "annual addition" limit (discussed in chapter 7).

loan.)[2] Third, dividends that are reinvested in company stock at the direction of participants are also tax-deductible. (Note that such an election by participants may require compliance with federal and/or state securities laws.)

Dividend deductions are not subject to the 25% limit described above for ESOP contributions because dividends are not company contributions. Rather, they are investment income paid on the ESOP-held shares. To be deductible, dividends must be "reasonable." Additionally, they are not deducted from the corporation's income when computing the alternative minimum tax.

S corporations do not pay dividends for tax purposes, and so no deduction is needed or available. However, S corporation shareholder distributions are generally considered dividends under state corporate law. When these distributions are paid, usually to allow non-ESOP shareholders to pay their taxes on S corporation income, the ESOP must receive a pro-rata share of the distribution, which it retains as earnings because an ESOP is a tax-exempt trust. (See chapter 6, "ESOPs for S Corporations.")

Deferring taxation using the Section 1042 "rollover." Providing for business continuity is one of the most difficult challenges for closely held companies. Even if buyers can be found, the terms of their offers may not be acceptable, either financially or personally. For example, a buyer may want to shut down the company or eliminate valued employees. As hard as it is to sell a business outright, it is even harder to sell it in stages, allowing for a gradual withdrawal by the owner; or partially, allowing heirs, key managers, or others to have a partial ownership interest.

An ESOP provides a way to accomplish these goals in a tax-advantaged manner and manage the sale process more effectively. First, as described above, the ESOP allows the company to use pretax dollars to buy out the owners. This can be done under whatever schedule is practical. Second, the seller(s) can defer capital gains taxation on the sale proceeds.

Under Section 1042 of the Internal Revenue Code (the "Code"), an owner of a closely held C corporation can indefinitely defer capital gains taxation on stock he or she sells to an ESOP if (1) after the sale the ESOP owns 30% or more of each class of outstanding stock or of the total value of

---

2. This restriction applies to stock bought by an ESOP after August 4, 1989.

all outstanding stock, excluding nonconvertible, nonvoting preferred stock; and (2) the seller reinvests ("rolls over") the sale proceeds into "qualified replacement property" (QRP) during the period from three months before to twelve months after the sale. The selling shareholder in a Section 1042 transaction can be an individual, a trust,[3] an estate, a partnership, or a limited liability company (LLC). However, neither a C nor (probably) an S corporation can sell to an ESOP and elect Section 1042 treatment.

Qualified replacement property (QRP). QRP includes stocks, bonds, or other securities of operating corporations[4] incorporated in the U.S. It does not include, for example, government bonds, mutual funds, real estate investment trusts (REITs), or ownership through means other than a security (e.g., a partnership interest). Not surprisingly, QRP also does not include securities from the very company that issued the securities sold to the ESOP or from a member of the same controlled group of corporations.

The money "rolled over" into QRP need not be the actual proceeds from the sale, but rather can be an equivalent amount of money from another source. Some or all of the proceeds can be rolled over. The seller(s) will simply pay taxes on the rest. Two or more owners may combine their sales to meet the 30% requirement if the sales are part of a single, integrated transaction. It has become increasingly common in Section 1042 transactions for sellers to facilitate the sale by pledging part or all of their QRP as collateral for the loan, especially in companies with limited assets or with substantial debt.

Nonallocation rule. In a transaction to which Section 1042 applies, none of the shares sold to the ESOP may be allocated to ESOP accounts of the seller; certain relatives of the seller (ancestors, siblings, the spouse, or lineal

---

3. A trust can sell to an ESOP and elect Section 1042 where it is the taxpayer (e.g., not a revocable grantor trust).

4. An "operating corporation" is one where more than 50% of the assets were used in the active conduct of its business either when the securities were purchased or before the 15-month period for buying QRP ended. No more than 25% of the operating corporation's income can come from passive investment income. Regardless of these rules, banks defined as such under Code Section 581 and insurance companies subject to taxation specifically qualify as "operating corporations" for this purpose.

descendants); other sellers who elect Section 1042 treatment; shareholders owning more than 25% of company stock;[5] or family members of more-than-25% shareholders if they own stock by attribution (e.g., spouses).

The prohibition on allocations extends to direct or indirect allocations under any qualified plan of the employer (such as "make-up" contributions of an equivalent amount of cash in the ESOP or another qualified plan). For sellers electing Section 1042 treatment and their affected relatives, the prohibition begins on the day the shares are sold to the ESOP and ends on the later of (1) the date 10 years after the sale or (2) if the sale was financed with a loan, the date of the final allocation of shares to participants after the debt is repaid. For more-than-25% shareholders and those who hold such shareholders' stock by attribution, the prohibition lasts forever.

There is one exception to this nonallocation rule: lineal descendants of the selling shareholder(s) may be allocated a total of 5% of the stock, provided that the lineal descendants are not treated as more-than-25% shareholders by attribution.

This nonallocation rule does not apply to other ESOP-held stock that was purchased from a seller who did not elect Section 1042 treatment.

Other requirements. There are other requirements for the Section 1042 rollover. For example, the selling shareholder(s) must have held the stock for at least three years before the sale. However, if a seller received the stock as a gift or acquired it in a tax-free exchange (e.g., a partnership interest converted to stock when the partnership incorporated) the three-year holding period includes the prior holding period of the donor or of the partnership interest. The seller cannot have received the stock through exercising stock options, a distribution from a qualified retirement plan (such as the ESOP itself), or restricted stock or discounted stock purchase arrangements under Section 83 of the Code. If the ESOP

---

5. For purposes of this rule, owning more than 25% of the company is broadly defined. "More than 25%" includes, for example, owning more than 25% of any class of stock of (or more than 25% of the value of) any member of the same controlled group of corporations. Ownership includes not only stock itself but also the value of stock that would be acquired through the exercise of options and similar equity instruments. Finally, ownership by certain related parties such as parents and spouses is counted.

disposes of the shares within three years after the sale, the employer generally must pay a 10% excise tax on the proceeds from the disposition. There are three procedural requirements the seller must meet:

1. The seller must affirmatively elect Section 1042 treatment in a "statement of election" attached to the seller's tax return.

2. The seller must file with the statement of election a "statement of consent" from the employer corporation consenting to the imposition of excise taxes if the ESOP's three-year holding period mentioned above is violated, or if a prohibited allocation is made.

3. For each purchase of QRP (see above), the seller must file a notarized "statement of purchase."

If a selling shareholder who has elected Section 1042 treatment sells or disposes of any QRP, he or she will pay tax (except in certain cases such as a charitable contribution).[6] Sellers using the Section 1042 rollover can avoid taxation completely by retaining the QRP until death, at which time the property transfers to their heirs with a stepped-up basis.

The Section 1042 tax deferral is not available for selling shareholders in S corporations.

The S corporation ESOP tax advantage. As discussed in the chapter on ESOPs for S corporations, an ESOP in an S corporation is not subject to federal income tax on its share of the corporation's net income. Most state tax laws mirror this provision. Although S corporations do not pay tax on their profits, they generally pay distributions to their shareholders to fund the shareholders' liability for taxes on their proportionate share of corporate profits. Thus, when an ESOP wholly owns an S corporation, no distributions need be paid out to fund payments for federal (and often state) taxes. This provides an indirect but often very substantial tax benefit.

---

6. It is important to remember that the QRP is *not* like a tax-deferred account such as an IRA within which the account holder can buy and sell without paying any tax. Instead, the seller must make his or her investment decisions within 12 months after the ESOP transaction and then either stick with those decisions or dispose of the QRP (or part of it) and pay taxes. As stated above, there are exceptions to taxation, such as when the QRP is donated to a charity.

CHAPTER 4

Uses of ESOPs

Aside from their obvious use as a tax-advantaged way of providing an employee benefit, ESOPs have a variety of special applications, such as the following.

For business continuity. The most common use of an ESOP is to sell part or all of an owner's interest in a closely held company. In this situation, an ESOP provides substantial advantages over other alternatives:

- It provides a ready market for the stock.

- The company can fund the transaction with pretax dollars.

- The owner(s) may sell to the ESOP partially, or in stages over a period of years so they can gradually ease out of the company—a particularly important consideration for sellers with management responsibilities.

- In a C corporation, the selling owner(s) may defer taxation on the gains by using the Section 1042 "rollover" explained above.

- In an S corporation, distributions that would otherwise be used for shareholders to pay taxes on S corporation income may be used to fund a portion of the ESOP share purchase.

As a tool of corporate finance. A leveraged ESOP can be used to borrow money that could be used to buy another company or new equipment, or to refinance debt. To accomplish these goals, the company issues new shares and sells them to the ESOP in a leveraged transaction, using the proceeds from the sale of new shares to finance acquisitions or to refinance debt. The company raises new capital by allowing the ESOP to buy new shares; this is funded by corporate contributions to the ESOP that come from pretax company cash flow. While this dilutes the ownership of the non-ESOP shareholders, it allows a much less costly repayment of the loan and simultaneously provides an employee benefit plan. If properly structured, the corporation's growth due to the additional capital will exceed the dilution caused by issuing new shares.

Either the ESOP borrows money or, more commonly, the company borrows money and relends it to the ESOP. The ESOP then buys stock from the company, which repays the loan and deducts both the principal and the interest. Companies have used leveraged ESOPs to refinance debt, buy stock back from a public market, acquire assets or other companies, and buy out owners.

To spread corporate ownership among all employees. Many business owners, managers, and employees philosophically believe in spreading ownership as broadly as possible. The tax and other advantages noted above are simply icing on the cake for them. Some companies have no owners who wish to sell; such companies fund their ESOPs not by buying out existing owners but simply by contributing shares as a way to reward and motivate employees.

As a match to a 401(k) plan. Many employers now use ESOP contributions to match pretax employee contributions to 401(k) plans. The matching contribution can be made at the typical matching rate, funded in company stock.[1] This ESOP may also be used to fund a "safe harbor" 401(k) with company stock instead of cash. For example, employers who provide fully vested across-the-board contributions equaling at least 3% of pay or more to a 401(k) or other defined contribution plan, or who provide fully vested matching contributions of 100% of employee deferrals up to 3% of pay and 50% for the next 2% of pay, do not have to meet all the strict testing rules for employee deferrals to 401(k) plans. An ESOP is one defined contribution plan that can be used to provide these contributions. The ESOP and 401(k) plan can operate side by side, or they can be integrated into a single plan to achieve this plan design. Moreover, if an employer is already paying dividends on employer shares held by a 401(k) plan, placing these shares in an ESOP can make these dividends

---

1. Note that combined or coordinated ESOPs and 401(k) plans of public companies are subject to significant additional diversification and disclosure requirements.

tax-deductible if the dividends are passed through to participants or reinvested in company stock at the direction of participants.

To build a stronger corporate culture. Studies have shown that simply implementing an ESOP does not by itself typically increase corporate
performance. When ownership is not broadly shared, introducing "participative management"—in which rank-and-file employees participate
in decisions affecting their jobs through such means as work teams, total
quality management, or employee task forces—has only a small positive
effect. However, companies that *combine* employee ownership (as through
an ESOP) and participative management tend to show substantial gains
in performance, growing 6% to 11% per year faster than would otherwise
be expected.

In 2000, in the largest and most significant study to date on the performance of ESOPs in closely held companies, Douglas Kruse and Joseph
Blasi, both of Rutgers University, found that ESOPs increased sales, employment, and sales per employee by about 2.3% to 2.4% per year over
what would have been expected absent an ESOP. ESOP companies also
were somewhat more likely to still be in business several years later.

A 2010 NCEO study found that company contributions to ESOPs
were on average 75% higher than their contributions to non-ESOP defined contribution plans. A 1998 study in Washington State found that
ESOP companies provided significantly higher retirement benefits than
non-ESOP companies, that these higher benefits did not come at the
cost of lower wages, and that employees in ESOP companies had approximately as much in diversified retirement assets as did employees in
non-ESOP companies.

Other uses. In rare cases, ESOPs have been used as a takeover defense
or to save a distressed company. While these are among the most publi-
cized applications, they require very special circumstances to be success-
ful.

CHAPTER 5

Valuing the Company Stock

Valuation is one of the most important ESOP issues. The ESOP cannot pay more than fair market value for stock it acquires, and in a closely held company, all transactions involving company stock must be based on a valuation from an independent appraiser. There is a potential conflict of interest here, especially when the ESOP trustee (who is responsible for determining that the ESOP is not paying more than fair market value for the stock) is a selling shareholder who would benefit from a high price,[1] but the ESOP and its participants would benefit from a lower price.[2] Given this conflict and the effect valuation has on the benefits participants receive from the ESOP, it is not surprising that many ESOP-related lawsuits involve valuation. The basic rules are as follows:

1. *The stock must be valued at least annually, and as needed for transactions.* The laws and regulatory authority governing ESOPs require that all assets held by an ESOP, not just company stock, be valued at least once per year. Even if there are no transactions during the year, that value is used for the participants' account statements and for the ESOP's Form 5500 annual report filed with the U.S. Department of Labor. Additionally, stock must be valued when it is sold (or contributed) to the ESOP, which ensures that it will not pay more than fair market value. When employees are cashed out of their ESOP shares, the price they receive is the fair market value. ESOPs are often set up so that after the appraiser delivers the annual appraisal report, account statements are provided to employees and shares

---

1. A corporate officer who reports to a selling shareholder could also be in a conflicted situation, feeling pressure to give his or her boss "the right price" for the shares. If the company contributes stock directly to the ESOP, it too would benefit from a higher price because it would receive a greater tax deduction (assuming it is paying taxes and can thus use the deduction).

2. The conflict of interest is especially grave if the selling shareholder is also the trustee. For this reason, it is very unwise for the seller to become the trustee, even though it is not against the law.

are bought back from employees while the valuation is still "fresh." When some time has gone by since the valuation but a transaction must be made, the trustee must either be able to show the valuation is still current or engage the appraiser to affirm what fair market value now is.

2. *Closely held company stock must be valued by an independent appraiser.* In a public company (defined for these purposes as one whose securities are readily tradable on an established securities market), the value for ESOP purposes is simply the public market price. However, most ESOP companies are closely held, and in such companies the valuation must be based on a report from an "independent" appraiser. This clearly means, for example, that the appraiser cannot have a financial interest in the company. It is not always clear where to draw the line, however. A CPA who audits the firm's financials for non-ESOP purposes is not independent, but what about someone from a large CPA firm who is in a different department from the person auditing the company's financials? What about someone who is affiliated with another ESOP advisor the company uses? People disagree about the answers to these questions, but the safest thing to do, and what we at the NCEO recommend, is to hire a completely independent appraisal firm with demonstrated expertise in valuing company shares for ESOP purposes. (Moreover, given how specialized the ESOP field is, it would be a coincidence for a company's CPA firm to have experience and expertise in conducting ESOP valuations.)

3. *The ESOP cannot pay more than "adequate consideration," i.e., fair market value, for the shares, and departing participants must receive fair market value for their shares.* "Fair market value" is defined as the price at which property would change hands in an arm's-length transaction between a willing seller and a willing buyer when they have no compulsion to buy or sell and both parties have reasonable knowledge of the relevant facts. ESOPs are generally financial buyers, not strategic or synergistic buyers. An ESOP cannot match the price offered by a synergistic buyer who would pay a premium over financial fair market value due to such synergies as added efficiencies after the sale

that would apply only to that buyer. Although the ESOP cannot pay company owners more than fair market value for their shares, the ESOP trustee should negotiate the best price it can get, which might be below fair market value.[3] (When ESOP participants receive share distributions and sell them back to the company or ESOP, they must receive full market value. It would be illegal and unfair to remaining participants to pay *more* than fair market value, which would effectively transfer corporate profits to the departing participants at the expense of the remaining ones.) Thus, the ESOP cannot pay more than fair market value under any circumstances, even if another potential buyer would do so (e.g., an investor who offers a premium to buy the company due to its synergistic value to him or her). Similarly, if the ESOP sells shares, it cannot receive less than fair market value for them. The trustee must arrive at the stock valuation in good faith based on the appraiser's report. This means the trustee cannot blindly accept the report but rather must conduct a sufficient investigation to satisfy himself or herself that the price given by the appraiser constitutes fair market value.

Approaches to valuing company stock. There are three basic approaches to business valuation:

1. The *asset approach* values the company by valuing its assets and liabilities. Because it ignores many factors bearing on the company's future profits, this approach is best suited to valuing companies that are highly asset-intensive (such as real estate holding companies) or companies that may be near a liquidation (i.e., to determine how much money could be gained from selling the company's assets) and is little used in valuation for ESOP purposes.

2. The *income approach* values the company by converting the expected income of the company to a value for its shares. This is often done by estimating future free cash flow and discounting it. This approach usually carries the most weight in the valuation.

---

3.   If the price were far below fair market value, a selling shareholder could hypothetically be liable for gift tax if the discounted sale were found to be a deemed gift, but in practice this is very rare.

3. The *market approach* values the company by looking at the trading prices of comparable public companies and/or the price paid in mergers and/or acquisitions of comparable companies. Previous sales of the company's own stock in arm's-length transactions may also be considered.

In any case, the appraiser cannot simply use a formula but rather must conduct a detailed investigation of the company (including an on-site visit and interviews with key personnel and perhaps others) and produce a report that explains its conclusions. The company will have to provide information such as financial statements, sales projections, budgets, compensation schedules, and so on. It is important for the company to provide complete and accurate information; misleading the appraiser (i.e., to get the seller a higher price) constitutes serious wrongdoing and is an invitation to investigations and lawsuits.

Discounts and premiums. Depending on various circumstances, the final conclusion of value for the shares being appraised can reflect discounts or premiums.

A controlling interest in a company is generally worth more than a minority (non-controlling) interest because it gives the shareholder the power to control the company. If a value for the shares is derived on a minority basis (for example, using the multiples of comparable public companies, which constitutes a minority interest) but the ESOP is buying a controlling interest in the company, then the final conclusion of fair market value will probably reflect a premium for control. If the ESOP is buying a minority interest in the company without control rights and the valuation was based on merged and/or acquired companies, a minority discount may be applied to adjust the valuation.[4]

If the valuation method begins with a value derived on a marketable basis, then a discount for lack of marketability (often in the range of 5% to 15%) may be applied to the shares of the closely held ESOP company.

---

4. Some appraisers and others argue that if the ESOP begins by buying a minority interest in the company but has the right to buy control in future transactions, then the ESOP can pay a control premium at each step along the way, given the right circumstances.

Some appraisers and others argue that this discount should be reduced or even eliminated on the grounds that ESOP participants have the right to sell their shares back to the company (creating the company's "repurchase obligation"). However, others disagree because, for example, the right to sell shares back to the company is a participant right, not a right of the ESOP, for which the valuation is being made. An adjustment to the value to reflect the repurchase obligation may be applied to change the lack-of-marketability discount or to another factor.

The post-transaction price drop. When a company borrows money to finance a leveraged ESOP transaction (as when the ESOP buys a large block of stock from shareholders), the debt it takes on goes on its balance sheet, thus reducing its value. Thus, immediately after the transaction, the company will be worth less than what the ESOP paid for it. This can be confusing for ESOP participants if the company does not explain that their benefit at the outset of the ESOP is not reduced by this drop because their first ESOP allocation is at the post-transaction value. Over time, as the debt is repaid, the value of the company's stock will rebound, all other things being equal. Moreover, the potential tax and employee productivity benefits from the ESOP can accelerate this rebound and make the company (and thus the ESOP participants' accounts) worth more than ever.

The company may adopt a floor price protection agreement (also called a "floor put") that compensates some or all departing participants for the price drop during a stated period of time, generally by paying them the difference between the price they receive for their shares and the price they would have received but for the leveraged transaction. This would generally be done where the ESOP is already in place and a new leveraged transaction causes a decline in value due to the additional debt, causing departing participants to receive a smaller payout due to the post-transaction price drop.[5]

---

5.   By the time participants vest, build up enough in their ESOP accounts so the stock price has a significant impact on them, leave the company, and receive distributions after the original transaction, the stock price is likely to have recovered from the initial post-transaction price drop. With a subsequent transaction, participants will have been around long enough so that they might leave

Hiring an appraiser. As noted above, the company must hire an independent appraiser, and we at the NCEO recommend a truly independent one with no financial relation to the company or other parties to the transaction (such as the attorney or other advisors involved with the ESOP). The appraiser should be familiar with the issues raised by ESOPs. It is a good idea to speak to several appraisal firms before settling on one. Different appraisers have not only different levels of experience and different fees but also different philosophies about valuation. The goal, however, is not to find an appraiser who will give the selling shareholder(s) a "good deal" (again, the ESOP cannot pay more than fair market value) but rather to find a reliable expert who will accurately determine the value of the company's stock and whom the company can work with on an ongoing basis. Usually, the same appraiser used in the initial transaction will be hired for follow-up valuations in future years. (The follow-up appraisals will generally be at a lower price because the appraiser has already conducted a detailed initial investigation in producing the original appraisal.)

The company may pay the appraiser, but the appraiser's client is the ESOP; again, the appraiser is there to help protect the ESOP's interests by providing the trustee with a determination of fair market value.

---

and start receiving distributions while the post-transaction price drop from the subsequent transaction still drags down the value of their shares.

CHAPTER 6

ESOPs for S Corporations

An S corporation is one that elects to be taxed under Subchapter S of Chapter 1 of the Code. Among other requirements, the corporation can have no more than 100 shareholders (a number that has been raised over the years) and can have only one class of stock (however, different shares can have different voting rights). Unlike a C corporation, an S corporation does not pay tax on its profits. The profits or losses of an S corporation are divided up and passed through to its shareholders based on their individual ownership percentages. Each shareholder pays income tax on his or her portion of the income, usually with funds the S corporation distributes to them for this purpose. S corporations thus avoid the "double taxation" that occurs when C corporations are taxed at the corporate level and then distribute after-tax earnings to shareholders, who also pay taxes themselves.[1]

The ESOP is a single shareholder for S corporation purposes. Because the ESOP trust is the shareholder, not the employees, having an ESOP in itself does not violate the 100-shareholder limit, no matter how many employees the company has. Additionally, an S corporation ESOP need not offer participants the right to receive distributions in company stock, which protects it from violating the 100-shareholder limit.

Tax advantages and policy issues. The S corporation election alone, with the single taxation it brings, is attractive to many private companies. In addition, a major tax advantage has especially motivated many S corporations to set up ESOPs, and ESOP-owned C corporations to elect S corporation status: as a tax-exempt trust, an ESOP in an S corporation is not subject to federal income tax on its share of the corporation's net income. Most states mirror this provision. An ESOP provides an S corporation with the potential to retain much more of its earnings than it would otherwise. For example, take an S corporation with $3 million in

---

1. In some states, certain minimum or "franchise" taxes may apply to S corporation income, such as a franchise tax in California consisting of the greater of 1.5% of the corporation's net income or $800.

taxable income. Without an ESOP, the shareholders would collectively be responsible for perhaps $1 million or so of income tax. The company would normally make $1 million in distributions to shareholders to pay their taxes on their share of S corporation income. However, if an ESOP owns 100% of the company, that $1 million remains for the company to keep and use as it wishes.

When there are both ESOP and non-ESOP S corporation shareholders and the company makes a distribution to the non-ESOP shareholders to fund their tax payments, it must also make a pro-rata distribution to the ESOP based on its ownership percentage. Having an ESOP makes no difference in the corporation's responsibility to fund its shareholders' tax bills. Because an S corporation distribution is still a dividend under state law, all shareholders of the same class (and there is only one class of stock in an S corporation) have equal rights to distributions. Even though the non-ESOP owners might wish the ESOP did not have to receive such distributions, the cash flow advantages are still significant. S corporation distributions to the ESOP may be used to pay ESOP administration expenses, including annual appraisal and legal costs; fund benefit distributions, thus easing liquidity concerns at the corporate level; repay an ESOP loan; or buy more shares from sellers or the company. However, if the company wishes to pass through distributions to employees, as a C corporation might do with dividends on ESOP shares, the distribution from the ESOP would have to meet the "in-service" distribution rules for active employees. There are also early distribution excise tax and participant consent issues that may make it impractical, unlike the case with C corporation dividends, which can be distributed by the ESOP trustee without participant consent.

The S corporation election may be most compelling for an ESOP company when the ESOP owns all of the company. However, in all cases it nets additional cash flow that would otherwise be lost to federal income taxes (until ESOP benefits are paid out to participants).

Keep in mind that ESOP participants pay tax on their distributions from the plan. Thus, the S corporation ESOP tax exemption is not a tax dodge that completely removes S corporation income from the reach of the Internal Revenue Service (IRS). Rather, it shifts S corporation taxation from the immediate taxation of profits to the eventual taxation of the value of the stock accounts distributed to ESOP participants. To tax both the ESOP and the participants in an S corporation would arguably impose the double taxation that S corporations are statutorily designed to avoid.

Tax disadvantages. The "Section 1042" tax deferral (see "ESOP Tax Incentives," above) is not available for sales of S corporation stock to an ESOP. S corporation distributions paid on ESOP shares are not deductible (S corporation distributions are not dividends for tax purposes). Finally, interest payments on an ESOP loan are included under the 25% annual contribution limit. However, the use of S corporation distributions on ESOP-held stock to repay the loan can usually more than make up for the inclusion of interest in the 25% limit. S corporation distributions are not constrained by the "reasonableness" requirement attached to deductible C corporation dividends on ESOP shares.

Anti-abuse rules. When S corporations became eligible to have ESOPs in the late 1990s, tax-abusive schemes emerged. For example, one or a few highly paid individuals could incorporate as an S corporation, form an ESOP, transfer the stock to it, and thus avoid current taxation without providing the broad-based ownership that is the policy basis for ESOP tax benefits. "Anti-abuse" legislation enacted in 2001 (Section 409(p) of the Internal Revenue Code) attempted to curtail these abuses by effectively limiting the use of ESOPs in S corporations to situations where ownership of company stock through the ESOP is broad-based. In response, promoters of tax-avoidance schemes came up with arrangements such as "management company ESOPs." Such a scheme might work like this: Company A spins off Company B, an ESOP-owned S corporation employing some executives. Company B is paid most of Company A's profits as a management fee for running Company A. Thus, the profit produced by Company A's workers is siphoned off to enrich those at Company B.

In rulings and regulations interpreting the 2001 anti-abuse legislation, the IRS cracked down on these and other schemes. The anti-abuse rules as they now exist are complex, but in essence they work as follows: If "disqualified persons" own 50% or more of the outstanding shares of an S corporation that has an ESOP (counting shares held directly, "deemed-owned shares," and shares they are considered to own under the general attribution-of-ownership tax rules), then there is a "nonallocation year."

This means that the anti-abuse rules have been violated, and heavy tax penalties will be imposed.

- *Disqualified persons.* A "disqualified person" is anyone who owns 10% or more of the "deemed-owned shares" of the company (see below) or with his or her family collectively owns 20% or more of the deemed-owned shares. The disqualified person test is performed both ignoring "synthetic equity" and counting synthetic equity in the test (see below). Similarly, the 50%-plus ownership test is performed both ignoring synthetic equity and counting synthetic equity owned by disqualified persons to see whether a nonallocation year occurs.

- *Deemed-owned shares.* The "deemed-owned shares" do not include direct stock ownership. They include forms of equity that are not actual shares. Namely, deemed-owned shares include company shares allocated to someone's ESOP account, and ESOP-owned company shares that are presently unallocated but will be allocated to that account as the ESOP loan is paid off. They also include "synthetic equity," which is broadly defined to include stock options, warrants, phantom stock, stock appreciation rights, restricted stock, certain deferred compensation arrangements, and other rights to acquire stock or assets, if such equity will make someone a disqualified person.

During a nonallocation year, disqualified persons may not receive allocations, which are defined as (1) "accruals" (meaning that S corporation shares held by the ESOP, or assets attributable to it, are held for their benefit) or (2) "allocations" (meaning any allocation under the ESOP, or any allocation under any other tax-qualified plan of the employer that, but for a provision in the ESOP precluding such an allocation, would have been added to a disqualified person's ESOP account and invested in company stock). Tax penalties are imposed both on allocations (including "accruals") and on synthetic equity included in the definition of "deemed-owned shares." A prohibited allocation may also disqualify the ESOP itself.

Note that the anti-abuse rules target disproportionate ownership not only by ESOP participants but also by non-participants who own synthetic equity. For example, the rules will be violated if an S corporation with an ESOP has a non-employee holding stock options that would give him or her 50% of the company if exercised. Aside from this, a more general effect of the rules is that it is difficult to establish a 100% ESOP in a very small S corporation, especially one with 10 or fewer employees. Given 10 participants in a 100% ESOP-owned S corporation, for example, it is likely that at least 50% or more of the shares will be owned by disqualified persons (for example, five or more participants each having 10% or more of the shares allocated or deemed to be allocated to their accounts), thus resulting in a nonallocation year.

Making the S corporation ESOP decision. Due to the absence of several ESOP tax incentives available to C corporations—the Section 1042 tax deferral, dividend deductions, and higher contribution limits (due to the exclusion of interest payments on an ESOP's loan from the 25% deduction limit)—ESOPs are often set up in S corporations where the employer and selling shareholders have different motivations and objectives than their C corporation counterparts. Historically, the growth in the number of ESOPs in closely held companies was driven by selling shareholders deferring tax on the sale (through the Section 1042 "rollover") and the company deducting as much as it could through ESOP contributions under the 25% limit and by using deductible dividends. Many sellers today, however, decide that given the historically low capital gains tax rates, they would prefer to pay capital gains taxes now rather than defer them to a point in the future when the rates may be higher.

Selling shareholders in an S corporation often are those who are not concerned about getting the tax deferral or who are motivated by the tax savings to the company and the more rapid repayment of ESOP loans that can occur in an S corporation ESOP. For example, if the ESOP purchases 100% of the company's shares in a single transaction, all of the cash flow that would otherwise be used to pay federal and state income tax (after the 25% of covered payroll deduction) may be used to repay the ESOP loan. This can reduce the loan amortization period by up to 30%. If 50% of the shares are purchased, then 50% of these funds that otherwise would be used for taxes may be used for ESOP debt service.

These tax advantages make the ESOP-owned S corporation a much more efficient capital structure both during the transaction and after the sale is completed. Larger-percentage ESOP transactions are much more compelling in an S corporation setting. S corporation ESOPs typically reach a larger percentage of company share ownership faster than their C corporation counterparts. Additionally, many mature ESOP-owned C corporations have elected S status to take advantage of the tax exemption for the ESOP's share of S corporation earnings.

For selling shareholders who place a high value on the tax advantage of the 1042 rollover transaction, it is possible to set up an ESOP in a C corporation, allow the selling owner(s) to make the Section 1042 election, and then convert the company to S status to gain the advantages discussed above. It is also possible for an S corporation to revoke its S corporation election and convert to C status so the selling owner(s) can elect the Section 1042 tax deferral. The company can later re-elect S status, but only after five years. It is important to note that this five-year waiting period may not be unduly burdensome because a leveraged ESOP transaction may take up to five years to be paid off, during which time the company's tax liability may be reduced by the deductible ESOP funding.

However, if the S corporation shareholders have a high "basis" in their shares, they would pay much less in capital gains taxes, making the Section 1042 election less compelling (especially given the historically low capital gains tax rates at present). S corporation shareholder basis is highest in S corporations that are only distributing sufficient cash to allow shareholders to pay their taxes, typically 30 to 50 cents per dollar of taxable income. Shareholders will therefore accumulate basis each year at the rate of 50% to 70% of the S corporation's taxable income. Some S corporations will distribute much of their taxable income each year in cash, leaving their shareholders with a low basis, similar to that of C corporation shareholders that do not increase their basis each year. This is more likely to occur in non-capital-intensive S corporations, such as consulting or engineering firms as compared to manufacturing companies.

Making the decision to elect S corporation status as an ESOP company, or for an S corporation shareholder to decide to sell to an ESOP in an S corporation versus a C corporation, involves a number of issues that should be explored with a company's advisors. In addition to the issues discussed above, electing S status may trigger certain corporate-level taxes. Finally, the impact of the ESOP anti-abuse rules must be carefully evaluated by applying the anti-abuse tests, not simply after an ESOP is established but rather starting at the feasibility study stage, to avoid costly violations.

CHAPTER 7

Contribution and Allocation Limits

ESOPs are subject to limits on both the total amount of deductible contributions the company makes to the plan and on the amount allocated to each participant's account. Factors such as the presence or absence of other qualified retirement plans affect the limits for ESOP contributions and allocations in any particular case.

Limits on overall contributions to the plan. Generally speaking, all employer (but not employee) deductible contributions to defined contribution plans (including the ESOP, profit-sharing plans, 401(k) plans, and so on) are counted toward a single 25% limit under Section 404 of the Internal Revenue Code. However, recent IRS private letter rulings (PLRs) state that in a C corporation with a leveraged ESOP, there are separate 25% limits for (1) employer contributions to repay the principal on an ESOP loan and (2) employer contributions to other defined contribution plans or to a non-leveraged component of the ESOP itself (i.e., payments to the ESOP that are not used to pay either principal or interest on an ESOP loan).[1] Thus, a C corporation with a leveraged ESOP has a total 50% contribution limit available to it. This combined 50% limit is rarely used because most corporations do not wish to add benefits in excess of the loan-acquired shares.

Section 404 provides that the company cannot make any deductible contributions that, when allocated to participants, exceed the allocation limits under Section 415 discussed on the following pages.

Covered payroll. The "covered payroll" used in calculating the amount that can be contributed includes all currently taxable W-2 compensation, plus employee deferrals to 401(k) and cafeteria plans, for ESOP participants, who usually include all full-time employees aged 21 or over with at least one year of service. "Compensation" excludes any pay over $255,000 (as of 2013; this limit is indexed for inflation).

---

1. PLRs 200436015 (2004) and especially 200732028 (2007).

Payments outside the contribution limits. In C corporations, two sources of funds are not included in the 25% contribution limit(s):

- Dividends paid on ESOP-held company stock (because they are not contributions but rather earnings on the ESOP's assets). See chapter 3, "ESOP Tax Incentives," regarding dividend deductibility.

- Contributions to pay interest on a leveraged ESOP's loan.

In S corporations, distributions paid on ESOP-held shares, including distributions used to repay an ESOP loan, are not included in the single 25% limit on deductible contributions. However, contributions used to pay interest on a loan for a leveraged ESOP in an S corporation are included in calculating the 25% limit.

Nature of contributions. These contributions are not payroll deductions but rather separate payments by the employer that equal a certain percentage of payroll. Although an ESOP may allow participants to contribute to their own accounts, this occurs primarily in publicly traded companies because it raises bothersome securities law issues in closely held companies.

Limits on allocations to individual participants. Under Section 415 of the Internal Revenue Code, the "annual additions" to an individual participant's account under the ESOP and any other defined contribution plans cannot exceed the lesser of $51,000 (in 2013, as indexed for inflation) or 100% of his or her compensation. These "additions" include employer contributions, employee contributions,[2] and (except as noted below) reallocated forfeitures from participants who depart before they are vested. They do not include C corporation dividends or S corporation distributions paid on company stock, which are not considered "annual additions."

In C corporations, provided that not more than one-third of the company's ESOP contributions are allocated to "highly compensated employees," the following are not considered "annual additions" and are not counted

---

2. The annual addition limits do not, however, include employee deferrals in the form of "catch-up" contributions to 401(k) and other plans with elective salary deferrals, which such plans can allow for employees aged 50 and over.

against the allocation limits: (1) allocations resulting from contributions to pay interest on a leveraged ESOP's loan; and (2) shares purchased with a loan and allocated to a participant's account that are forfeited after the participant leaves the company before being fully vested and are then reallocated to other participants' ESOP accounts before the loan is fully repaid.

Note: In a leveraged ESOP, where payments on the loan cause shares to be released from the suspense account and allocated to employee accounts, the amount used in calculating the annual addition is generally not the value of the shares added to the employee's account but rather the amount used to repay the loan for that percentage of the shares. It is calculated based on either principal only or both principal and interest (the company chooses one or the other method for a given loan, within certain limits). For example, in a given year, the ESOP may repay 20% of the amount due on the loan and release a corresponding 20% of shares bought in the transaction from the suspense account. Using the principal-only method to illustrate the effect on an individual ESOP account, if the share price has doubled since the date of the ESOP transaction, a participant earning $51,000 (and thus able to receive up to a $51,000 allocation in 2013) may receive an allocation of stock worth $102,000 for which $51,000 in principal was repaid that year.

In the example above, if the share value has fallen since the ESOP transaction, the participant's account would actually receive less than $51,000 worth of shares, and participants might feel shortchanged by receiving shares that are worth less than what the company contributes to the plan.[3] In such a situation, it is possible to calculate annual additions using the actual value of the shares if the ESOP was designed to allow this.

Defined contribution plans such as ESOPs do not need to be aggregated with defined benefit plans in these calculations.

If too much is contributed or allocated. If the company contributes more than it can deduct, it is subject to excise taxes on the excess amount. However, if it contributes more than can be allocated, the plan may be subject to disqualification.

---

3.   In contrast, when C corporation dividends or S corporation distributions (which are not counted as "annual additions") paid on allocated shares are used to repay the ESOP loan, the value of the shares released from the suspense account and allocated to participants must at least equal the dividend or distribution.

CHAPTER 8

Employee Coverage and Entitlement to Benefits

ESOPs must meet certain rules to qualify for the tax incentives described above. Many of these rules are the same ones that apply to other qualified benefit plans.

Coverage. An ESOP is a broad-based program. Usually, all full-time employees aged 21 or over with at least one year of service participate. The following groups of employees may be excluded:

- Nonresident aliens;
- Employees in a separate line of business with 50 or more employees; and
- Employees covered by collective bargaining agreements, provided that retirement benefits have been the subject of good-faith collective bargaining.

Companies limiting participation beyond the guidelines enumerated above must heed the rules for participation and coverage. Excepting the three categories described above, a minimum percentage of employees aged 21 or over who have completed a year of service that includes 1,000 hours must benefit under the ESOP. The minimum percentage for coverage may be defined under one of three alternative tests:[1]

1. At least 70% of non-highly compensated employees are covered;
2. The percentage of non-highly compensated employees covered is at least 70% of the percentage of highly compensated employees covered; or
3. Any classification that does not discriminate in favor of highly compensated employees, as long as the average benefit percentage (which

---

1. If these coverage tests are not met, the plan is not disqualified, but the "highly compensated employees" (a term with a specific legal definition) will be taxed on their vested benefits and the income on those benefits.

35

generally is the average percentage of an employee's pay contributed to ESOPs and similar plans) for non-highly compensated employees is at least 70% of the average benefit percentage for highly compensated employees.

Allocation of ESOP shares. Shares must be allocated among participants based on their relative compensation or some other formula that does not discriminate in favor of highly compensated employees. The portion of any employee's salary that exceeds $255,000 (as of 2013; this amount is adjusted yearly for inflation) is ignored in this calculation. As noted in chapter 7 under "ESOP Tax Incentives," there are restrictions on allocating stock bought by the ESOP in a transaction to which Section 1042 applies. Furthermore, allocations are subject to the limits noted above under "Contribution and Allocation Limits."

Vesting and forfeitures. Vesting refers to the amount of time an employee must work before acquiring a nonforfeitable entitlement to his or her benefit. Employees who leave the company before being fully vested will forfeit their benefits to the extent they are not vested in them. An employee must become 100% vested when he or she reaches "normal retirement age" as defined in the Code. Additionally, an ESOP must comply with one of the following two minimum schedules for vesting (plans may provide different standards if they are more generous to participants):

- No vesting at all in the first years, followed by a sudden 100% vesting after not more than three years of service ("cliff" vesting); or
- Twenty percent vesting after the second year of service, with 20% more each year until 100% vesting occurs after the sixth year of service ("graded" vesting).

Pre-2007 rules allowed up to five years for cliff vesting and three to seven years for graded vesting. If the ESOP had a loan (incurred to buy company stock) that was outstanding as of September 25, 2005, a company may still use the pre-2007 rules during the loan's repayment period.

A "year of service" generally refers to a plan year in which a participant has 1,000 hours of service; it may include past service.

When departing employees leave before they are fully vested in their accounts, the amount that is not vested is generally forfeited. It is usually reallocated to remaining participants and may limit the amount of other contributions that can be allocated to such participants. Forfeitures may be used for administrative costs in rare situations. Note: if the company lays off 20% or more of the participating employees in the ESOP in a 12-month period, there may be a "partial termination" of the plan, requiring each of the affected participants to be 100% vested in the ESOP instead of forfeiting unvested amounts.

ESOP contributions designed to meet the 401(k) safe harbor tests must vest immediately, as with any contributions meant to meet those tests.

Diversification. In a retirement plan context, diversification is a plan participant's right to spread his or her account balance among different investments to decrease the participant's overall investment risk. For all private company ESOPs and for public company ESOPs that are not combined with a 401(k) plan, the rules are as follows: After ESOP participants reach age 55 and have participated in the plan for ten years, they have the right during the following five years to diversify up to a total of 25% of company stock that was acquired by the ESOP after December 31, 1986, and has been allocated to their accounts. During the sixth year, they may diversify up to a total of 50%, minus any previously diversified shares. To satisfy the diversification requirement, the ESOP must offer at least three alternative investments under either the ESOP or another plan such as a 401(k) plan, or distribute cash or company stock to the participants.

Since 2007, a different set of rules has governed public company ESOPs that are combined with a 401(k) plan. All participants can diversify their own contributions at any time, and participants who have three years of service can diversify all employer contributions.

Anti-cutback rules. Under the "anti-cutback" rules that apply to qualified plans such as ESOPs, accrued benefits cannot be reduced or eliminated except under certain conditions. With ESOPs, there are circumstances under which benefits in cash may be substituted for distributions in stock and under which the timing and form of distributions may be changed in a nondiscriminatory manner.

CHAPTER 9

Distributing Proceeds to the Participants

Distributions after leaving employment. The special rules for ESOP distributions provide that when employment terminates because the participant attains the normal retirement age under the plan, becomes disabled, or dies, the ESOP must begin to distribute vested benefits during the plan year following the event. When employment terminates for other reasons, such as when an employee quits, distribution must start no later than the sixth plan year after the plan year in which termination occurred (unless the participant is re-employed by the same company before then).

Under the special ESOP rules, distributions may be made in a lump sum or in substantially equal payments (not less frequently than annually) over a period no longer than five years (i.e., six payments over five years).[1] Distributions are made in the form of cash or stock.

If the ESOP is leveraged and in a C corporation, the plan may delay the commencement of distributions of shares acquired through the loan until the plan year after the plan year in which the ESOP loan is fully repaid. (It is unclear from the wording of the law whether S corporations can make this delay, but many S corporations do so without the IRS objecting. A 2010 NCEO survey found that 23% of S corporation ESOPs and 41% of C corporation ESOPs delay distributions until the ESOP loan has been repaid.[2]) Such delayed distributions must be completed by the later of (1) the end of the plan year after the plan year in which the loan is repaid or (2) the date distributions would be completed under the rules in the two paragraphs above.

---

1. This period may be extended when the account balance is very large: As of 2013, an ESOP distribution may be extended one year (up to a total of five additional years) for each $205,000 or fraction thereof that the participant's benefit exceeds $1,035,000 (these dollar amounts are indexed for inflation).

2. Chapter 7 of *The ESOP Repurchase Obligation Handbook* (Oakland, CA: NCEO, 2011) discusses these survey results in detail.

Regardless of the special ESOP rules, the general qualified retirement plan rules provide that a plan must (unless the participant chooses otherwise) begin distributing benefits no later than the 60th day after the end of the plan year in which the latest of the following events occurs: (1) attaining the earlier of age 65 or the plan's normal retirement age; (2) reaching the 10th anniversary of participation in the plan; or (3) terminating service. Additionally, there are rules governing distributions after death. Another general retirement plan rule requires minimum distributions to begin no later than the April 1 after the calendar year in which (1) more-than-5% owners of the company turn 70½, or (2) for others, the later of when the participant turns 70½ or retires.

Where the special ESOP rules and the general retirement plan rules conflict, the rule that produces an earlier distribution prevails. Usually this means the special ESOP rules, which do not make the participant wait until retirement age, but sometimes the general rules provide for an earlier distribution. For example, if someone with 10 years of ESOP participation quits at age 64, the special ESOP rules would allow the company to wait six years to commence distributions, but the general rules mandate distribution beginning at age 65 (or age 64 if the plan's normal retirement age is earlier than 65). Similarly, if the ESOP is still repaying the loan in this example, the special ESOP rules would allow distributions to be delayed during the years of repayment (in a C corporation), but the general rules override that.

Note: The special ESOP rules apply only to stock the ESOP acquired after 1986. An ESOP that was established before 1987 may still hold stock for which the plan is only obligated to follow the general retirement plan rules regarding distributions.

Distributions while participants are still employed. An ESOP is primarily a deferred income plan that provides employees with benefits after they terminate employment. However, in certain circumstances participants may receive benefits from the ESOP while they are still employed:

- As noted above, participants may "diversify" their accounts after a certain period and receive cash or stock directly.

- The employer, if it is a C corporation, may choose to pay dividends directly to participants on company stock allocated to their accounts, and it may pay dividends on company stock that has not been allocated to employee accounts directly to participants in the same proportion as the stock would be allocated to their accounts. In contrast, if the employer is an S corporation, paying distributions (the S corporation equivalent to dividends) directly to employees is not very practical because such distributions may be taxed unfavorably.

- As noted above, the plan must generally begin distributing benefits to a participant who is a more-than-5% owner after the participant reaches age 70½, even if the participant is still employed.

- There are certain other circumstances in which the plan may provide for in-service distributions, such as after a fixed number of years, upon attainment of a specified age, or upon "hardship."

Put option. Closely held companies that sponsor an ESOP must provide a "put option" on company stock distributed to participants by allowing them to sell the stock back to the company at its current fair market value. This duty is called the ESOP "repurchase obligation" (see chapter 13). At a minimum, the put option must be available during two periods, one for at least 60 days immediately following distribution and one for at least 60 days during the following plan year. Payment for shares sold under the put option must begin within 30 days after the participant exercises the option. If the participant exercises the put option for shares received as part of a distribution of his or her entire ESOP account within the span of one taxable year, the company can pay the amount over a period of up to five years, but it must provide adequate security and pay reasonable interest on the unpaid balance.

Privately held banks that are prohibited from buying their own securities can avoid providing a put option if participants can elect to take their distributions in cash.

The price paid to plan participants for their stock. In general, the price that participants receive for the company stock in their accounts will be the fair market value of the stock at the time the company (or ESOP) buys it back from them. For example, if the distribution is made in cash, the amount will equal the fair market value of the stock at that time. If the ESOP distributes shares in a lump sum and the company buys them back (under the put option discussed above) and pays the ex-employee in installments, the price will be the fair market value when the employee exercised the put option and the company bought the shares back. In contrast, if the ex-employee receives the distributions as installment payments from the ESOP (such as yearly payments for four years), the amount per share will be determined when each payment is made. Thus, if the stock price is rising (or falling) over time, with each installment, the ex-employee will receive more (or less) per share than he or she did before.

There is an exception to the rule that participants receive the fair market value of the company stock in their accounts. As the chapter on valuation explains, a company with a leveraged ESOP may establish a specified minimum price ("floor price") to be paid during the period of loan repayment when the value of the company stock is depressed by the loan, which protects departing participants from the post-ESOP transaction drop in value. (The company, not the ESOP, should pay the difference between fair market value and the floor price. There may be state law limitations that prevent an ESOP company from repurchasing such shares at the artificial floor price if the company cannot meet applicable balance sheet tests for corporate redemptions.)

Restrictions on transferring stock. Participants generally can sell company stock they receive from the ESOP to anyone, except that the plan may provide that the employer and the ESOP have rights of first refusal to match any offer received from a third party for such stock.

However, if the employer is a closely held company whose charter or bylaws restrict the ownership of substantially all (approximately 85%) of its stock to employees or a qualified plan, or if the employer is an S corporation, the ESOP (if the plan so provides) is not required to distribute stock; instead, it can distribute cash, or the employer can require the employee to sell distributed stock back to the employer.

Taxation of distributions. Employees pay no tax on stock allocated to their ESOP accounts until they receive distributions, at which time they are taxed on the distributions. If they are younger than age 59½ (or age 55 if they have terminated employment), they, like employees in qualified plans generally, are subject not only to applicable taxes but also to an additional 10% excise tax unless they roll the money over into an IRA or a successor plan in another company (or unless the participant terminated employment due to death or disability).[3]

ESOP distributions are generally taxed as ordinary income. However, employees who receive a lump-sum distribution of company shares will not be taxed (unless they so elect) on the net unrealized appreciation (NUA) of the shares—the appreciation in value of the stock while held by the plan. Instead, they will pay tax on the NUA only when they sell their shares, and at capital gains rates.[4] This can be a good strategy for some employees.[5] The NUA tax treatment is not available for shares rolled over into an IRA or an employee benefit plan.

If the money is rolled over into a traditional (not Roth) IRA or an employee benefit plan, the employee pays no tax until the money is withdrawn, at which point it is taxed as ordinary income. Distributions are immediately taxed as ordinary income if rolled over to a Roth IRA. Rollovers from ESOP distributions to IRAs are available for distributions of stock or cash over periods of less than 10 years.

When dividends are directly paid to plan participants on the stock allocated to their ESOP accounts, such dividends are fully taxable, although they are exempt from income tax withholding and are not subject to the excise tax that applies to early distributions. (As of this writing, it is

---

3. The 10% excise tax does not apply to deductible dividends that are passed through to participants, but it does apply to distributions made to participants as a result of their election of diversification (discussed in chapter 8).

4. The value of the shares when distributed is taxed at long-term capital gains rates, while any increase in value since distribution is taxed at short- or long-term capital gains rates, as appropriate.

5. The NUA strategy can be impossible (when participants do not receive lump-sum distributions of shares), impractical (when it is a private company that will no longer buy back the stock from the ex-employee after the "put option" periods have passed), or disadvantageous (when the company's stock price falls between the date of distribution and the date the ex-participant eventually sells the stock).

not established whether S corporation distributions to ESOP participants are subject to the excise tax.)

Participant consent; automatic rollovers. If the present value of an ESOP participant's benefit exceeds $5,000, the participant's consent must be obtained before a distribution is made unless the participant has reached the plan's normal retirement age (or has reached age 62 if the plan's normal retirement age is earlier than age 62). A distribution of more than $1,000 and not more than $5,000 made without the participant's consent must be automatically rolled over into an IRA unless the participant otherwise elects.

Anti-alienation rules. Generally speaking, a participant's account in a qualified retirement plan such as an ESOP cannot be assigned or alienated. In other words, neither the participant himself or herself nor a court can transfer ownership of the ESOP account or direct that the payment of benefits be made to someone else. This means, for example, that creditors cannot take away a participant's ESOP benefits, even in bankruptcy. However, there are exceptions to these anti-alienation rules. The main one is in the case of a qualified domestic relations order (QDRO) described below.

Qualified domestic relations orders (QDROs). As noted in the paragraph above, there is a general rule that participant accounts in qualified retirement plans such as ESOPs cannot be taken away from them. However, one exception is when a court (or other authorized governmental entity) issues a qualified domestic relations order (QDRO). A QDRO is an order providing that one or more persons other than the plan participant (persons such as an ex-spouse in a divorce) have the right to receive some or all of the plan benefits. Upon receipt of a domestic relations order, the plan must notify the participant and any payees under the order (such as a former spouse) of the order and the procedures to determine whether it is qualified (i.e., a QDRO), and then make the determination and notify the parties of the outcome within a reasonable period of time. The non-participant payees under the order are not subject to the 10% excise tax on early distributions mentioned above.

CHAPTER 10

Fiduciary Matters

Who is a fiduciary? Under the law, a fiduciary is someone who has a duty to act for the benefit of another with the highest standard of care, good faith, and honesty regarding the management of money or property. In the context of employee benefit plans such as ESOPs, ERISA defines a fiduciary as anyone who exercises any discretionary authority or control over managing the plan, exercises any authority or control over its assets, renders paid investment advice regarding its assets, or has any discretionary authority or responsibility regarding plan administration. This definition is broad and includes people such as plan administrators, trustees, investment managers, and in turn those who appoint others as fiduciaries. Additionally, ERISA requires every plan to have a "named fiduciary" who is specified in the plan or is indentified under a procedure given in the plan. ERISA requires plan fiduciaries not only to act in the exclusive interest of plan participants but also to act prudently. Failure to do so may result in legal liability under ERISA for losses.

ESOP fiduciary roles and responsibilities. An ESOP generally is governed by a trustee or administrative committee appointed by the board that assumes a fiduciary role with respect to operating the plan. Some of the many responsibilities may include determining that the price the ESOP pays for company stock is fair; that rules for allocation, vesting, distribution, and so on are carried out properly; and that plan assets are used to benefit the participants, not someone else.

Common fiduciary problems. Common fiduciary problems arise from improper valuations, imprudently purchasing shares for the ESOP with funds from a profit-sharing plan, buying more company stock when the fiduciary knows or should know that it is a poor investment, and discriminatory treatment of employees in paying their benefits.

Who can serve as a trustee? An ESOP trustee can be anyone, including a corporate officer or employee. It is safest to hire an independent fiduciary, which is often a bank trust department, but many closely held companies find the costs too high. Sellers can act as fiduciaries, but this puts them in an obvious conflict-of-interest situation, so it is better to have another corporate officer or employee assume this role if it is not filled by an outsider.

While the trustee or administrative committee acts as a fiduciary, this does not exclude other parties, such as the board or the top management of the company, from fiduciary duties if they make decisions concerning the operations of the plan. These obligations may seem onerous, but if trustees and management obtain qualified, experienced counsel; document their actions; and follow the often common-sense guidelines on how to set up a process for making sure the ESOP is operated fairly, the chances of being sued are remote. The most common problems are paying a price for stock that is more than the stock's fair market value and not paying people according to the requirements of the plan.

Who selects the trustee? ERISA specifically makes it the fiduciary duty of the company's board of directors to select, monitor, or remove the ESOP trustee and the ESOP "administrator" (the fiduciary administrator, not the recordkeeper for the plan, which generally is an outside third-party administrator [TPA]). Except where the sponsor company has become the ESOP administrator by failing to appoint a party to be the fiduciary administrator (not the TPA), this is the only fiduciary duty of the board of directors under ERISA and can be a trap for the unwary. If a company has outside independent directors, care should be taken to ensure that the board executes this duty carefully, since there is no corporate shield for fiduciary liability under ERISA. Normally, this is not a problem. However, if the board of directors becomes aware of a likely breach by a trustee, the board will have a fiduciary duty to remedy the breach.

CHAPTER II

The Rights of ESOP Participants

Voting rights. The ESOP trustee votes the ESOP shares. The ESOP participants must be given the right to direct how the trustee votes the shares in certain matters, as noted below; however, participants need not be given the right to decide whether to tender shares in response to a tender offer from a would-be buyer. Trustees sometimes hold the dual role of management and trustee. This generally is not a problem; however, the trustee must always be sure these actions do not violate standards of prudence and responsibilities to participants. Some companies have directed trustees, usually an outside firm that provides advice in ESOP decisions but is directed by another body, such as an ESOP fiduciary committee or the board. In these cases, the directing party is a fiduciary, but it is still the trustee who actually votes the shares.

In everyday practice this means that ESOPs do not have to change the way a company is governed, even if they own all the shares. Management or the board, for example, can still control the company. Companies that do give employees full voting rights, however, rarely find that this makes a great deal of difference in governance, because employees tend to be very conservative shareholders.

Publicly traded companies must allow ESOP participants to direct how company shares allocated to their accounts are voted on all matters. Closely held companies generally need only to give participants voting rights regarding a merger or consolidation, recapitalization, reclassification, liquidation, dissolution, or sale of substantially all of the assets of a trade or business of the company. The plan may either give participants the right to direct how the shares allocated to their accounts are voted or specify a one-vote-per-participant arrangement. These issues do not necessarily include the sale of stock, including all of a company's shares.

An ESOP may grant broader rights than the minimum outlined above. Closely held companies can give employees full voting rights, for example. Employees may also be given the right to decide whether to tender allocated *and* unallocated shares. In a leveraged ESOP, shares are allocated to participants' accounts as the loan that paid for them is paid off. This leaves unallocated shares that, under the minimum voting rights outlined above, may be voted by the fiduciary without regard to the participants' wishes. Many public company ESOPs have provided for "mirror voting and tendering," in which participants can direct the voting of unallocated shares in proportion to the voting of allocated shares; however, the U.S. Department of Labor argues that these voting directions cannot be binding on the ESOP trustee, and in one case a federal judge ruled in the Department of Labor's favor.

Information rights. The plan administrator must give plan participants a summary plan description (SPD) (a summary of the plan's provisions in easy-to-understand language) and a summary annual report disclosing the plan's assets and annual income or loss. Participants must be notified when they are eligible to receive benefits (including when they are eligible to roll over distributions into an IRA or other plan) and when they are eligible to diversify under the plan (see chapter 8). If the plan receives a domestic relations order, it must notify the affected participant (see chapter 9). At least once annually, the administrator must provide individual benefit statements. Within 30 days after a request in writing, participants must be given access to plan documents and any instruments under which the plan was established or is operated, and the Form 5500 annual report made to the government.

When (depending on the number of participants)[1] there is a certain percentage of participants who are literate only in the same non-English language, the SPD must include a notice in their language(s) offering assistance in their language(s) in understanding their rights and benefits under the plan.

Private company executives sometimes worry that installing an ESOP means disclosing confidential information to the world, but this is not true. The things that participants do *not* need to be provided in-

---

1. If the plan covers fewer than 100 participants in the plan at the beginning of the plan year, this requirement applies if 25% or more of all participants are literate only in the same non-English language. If the plan covers 100 or more participants at the beginning of the plan year, this requirement applies if the lesser of (1) 10% or more of all participants or (2) 500 or more participants are literate only in the same non-English language.

clude, for example, employee salaries, company financial information, the valuation report, the names and holdings of shareholders, and minutes of shareholder meetings. In other words, ESOP information rights are limited to information regarding the plan, its assets, and rights under the plan. However, communicating some things can be a good idea, such as discussing critical financial numbers as part of a participative management approach that invites all employees to focus on improving profitability (especially since they are now co-owners through the ESOP).

Claims and legal actions. Participants or beneficiaries who believe they have not received benefits to which they are entitled can file a claim with the plan. If the claim is denied, the participant is entitled to a written explanation, which the participant can appeal. If that appeal is denied, the participant can sue in federal court.

Aside from claims for benefits, participants and beneficiaries may also sue in federal court for improper conduct that breaches the fiduciary duties of one or more individuals or entities (as mentioned in chapter 10). An example is when the ESOP pays the selling shareholders too much for stock, thus leaving the participants with fewer shares than they deserve.

CHAPTER 12

Is an ESOP Right for Your Company?

Your corporate culture must be suited to, or adaptable to, employee ownership. If the employees at your company are not and will not be comfortable with the concept of employee ownership, an ESOP is not likely to work. For example, if managers refuse to treat subordinates as co-owners who have something to say about how their jobs are performed, the "employee owners" may feel cynical about the plan.

An ESOP may be too expensive if your company is too small. An ESOP will probably not be worthwhile for a company if the costs outweigh the economic and other advantages. A rule of thumb is that ESOPs work best for companies that are in the top corporate tax bracket (so they can take full advantage of the tax incentives) and have at least 20 employees and over $250,000 in payroll.

To set up an ESOP, a company with 20 employees may easily spend $50,000 to $70,000 or more on legal fees, stock valuation (assuming it is not publicly traded), and administrative costs. If the ESOP is even partially leveraged, fees easily increase by $20,000 or more. If equity investors or specialized debt is needed, expect to incur investment bankers' and/or loan fees. Administrative fees might start at $2,500 or more per year and increase with the number of participants. (One caveat: do not cut costs by hiring someone who does not specialize in ESOPs.) Ongoing fees, however, are much smaller, with total costs for small to mid-sized companies usually running between $15,000 and $30,000 per year.

Although it may cost more than $50,000 in fees for a leveraged ESOP to buy out an owner in a 20-employee company, the alternatives may be less desirable. A business broker's fee will probably exceed the cost of an ESOP transaction. If only a partial interest is for sale, it may be difficult to find a buyer willing to offer a reasonable price, provide adequate security, or offer continuing employment if the seller wants to remain with the company. Finally, the seller may simply want the employees to own the company.

Your payroll must be adequate. If you want to buy out an owner's interest in a company through a leveraged ESOP, it may be impractical if your covered payroll is too small relative to the value of the owner's interest. However, the tax law changes enacted in 2001 make it unlikely that this will be a problem in most cases.

- First, determine the covered payroll by taking all W-2 compensation, plus employee deferrals into 401(k) and cafeteria plans, excluding any employee's pay over $255,000 per year (as of 2013; this limit is indexed for inflation) and the pay of those who will not qualify for participation (e.g., part-time or short-term workers, or those excluded from allocations from stock bought in a Section 1042 "rollover" transaction, as explained above under "ESOP Tax Incentives").

- Second, to determine the maximum amount the company can contribute to the ESOP each year to repay the loan principal, multiply the covered payroll by 25%, which is the maximum deductible ESOP contribution. Subtract from that amount the total employer contribution (but not employee deferrals) to your 401(k) plan if you have one. In addition, no one employee can receive more than $51,000 (as of 2013, as indexed for inflation) or 100% of pay, whichever is less, in any one year from the combination of employer and employee contributions to defined contribution plans; any excess over this amount would need to be reallocated to other participants, if possible. Also, a reasonable amount of dividends used to repay the ESOP loan, as well as, in a C corporation, interest on the loan, may be added above the 25% limit.

- Finally, multiply this amount by the number of years in the loan (most bank loans to companies to fund ESOPs are for five to seven years) to determine how much you can borrow; alternatively, divide the amount you want to borrow by the amount you can contribute yearly to see how many years it will take to pay off the loan. If your yearly deductible contribution is too small to repay the loan, you generally can extend the term of the loan from the company to the ESOP to reduce the size of annual loan payments. Aside from this, consider whether the company will have enough cash flow to repay the loan.

An ESOP is unrealistic for many startup companies. For many start-ups, the costs of an ESOP may outweigh the benefits because they are not yet profitable and thus have no taxes on which to take ESOP deductions. Additionally, the owners may be uninterested in selling their stock and unwilling to have their shares diluted by issuing new stock. Such companies might instead consider using a 401(k) plan that includes company stock in the employer match, or granting stock options or other forms of equity compensation.

CHAPTER 13

Implementing and Administering an ESOP

Steps to setting up an ESOP. There are several steps to take when setting up an ESOP. The entire process typically takes from three to nine months for a leveraged ESOP, less for a nonleveraged one.

- The first step is to determine whether the owners—say, the owners of a closely held company, or the publicly traded parent company of a subsidiary whose employees want to organize a buyout—are ready to sell, or whether it is feasible for the company to issue new shares.

- Once that is determined, a feasibility study can be conducted by an outside consultant or in-house to determine whether the company is a good candidate for such a plan.

- Next, if the company is closely held, a qualified, independent appraiser should perform a preliminary valuation of the company and the portion of the stock that would be sold to the ESOP. (Later, a final valuation is performed when the transaction is closed.)

- A law firm with ESOP expertise then designs and drafts the ESOP plan document and submits it to the IRS. The plan document need not be filed with the IRS before the ESOP transaction. Although the plan can proceed from here, it should eventually obtain a favorable IRS "letter of determination."

- Next, the ESOP must be funded, whether by ongoing company contributions (in a nonleveraged plan), by a loan (in a leveraged plan), or by converting from an existing benefit plan such as a profit-sharing plan (see "Types of ESOPs," above). In closely held companies, the sellers themselves can finance the sale by taking back a note from the ESOP in exchange for their stock; however, this may prevent them from taking full advantage of the Section 1042 tax deferral. In some limited circumstances, an ESOP is funded by wage or benefit concessions from employees; this typically occurs when an ESOP is used to save a distressed company.

- A trustee or other fiduciary must be chosen to oversee the plan (see chapter 10). Most closely held companies use insiders, while most publicly traded companies use outsiders. In some cases, the company has an ESOP committee, usually drawn from management, that directs the trustee and oversees plan administration. The company will benefit greatly if it establishes a process to communicate the plan to employees that goes beyond the information required by law.

What employer stock may the ESOP own? In a publicly traded company, the common stock held by the ESOP must be readily tradable. In a closely held company, the ESOP must own common stock having a combination of voting and dividend rights at least equal to the class(es) of company common stock with the greatest voting power and dividend rights.

In both publicly traded and closely held companies, the ESOP also may own preferred stock that is convertible into the above-defined common stock at a reasonable conversion price. Whether common or preferred, the shares may come from authorized but unissued shares, treasury shares (stock held by the company), or shares owned by shareholders.

Ongoing administrative requirements. ESOPs have many administrative requirements, such as submitting various filings to the IRS and the U.S. Department of Labor; providing information to participants; and complying with a complex set of rules regarding contributions, allocations, distributions, forfeitures, diversification, repurchasing, and other matters regarding participants' accounts. To meet these and other requirements, companies generally have outside specialists provide record-keeping and administrative services for plans.

Repurchase obligation. As noted in chapter 9, closely held companies that sponsor ESOPs must provide a "put option" on company stock distributed to participants. This put option permits participants to require the company to repurchase the stock at its fair market value. The obligation to repurchase shares arises not only from distributions after termination of employment but also from in-service distributions and from diversification out of company stock while the participant is still in the plan. This obligation to repurchase shares is called the "repurchase obligation." It creates an emerging liability the company must plan to cover in order to avoid financial trouble in the future.

Accounting rules. The accounting rules for ESOPs are contained in Statement of Position 93-6 ("SOP 93-6"), which was developed by the American Institute of Certified Public Accountants and approved by the Financial Accounting Standards Board in 1993. SOP 93-6, which is effective for stock acquired by an ESOP in 1993 or later, provides that a leveraged ESOP's debt is recorded as a liability in the employer's financial statements whether or not the debt is guaranteed by the employer. (This added debt can lead to a decrease in share value after the ESOP is implemented.)

A contra equity account is set up as the offsetting entry; as the debt is repaid and shares are released from the suspense account to ESOP participants' accounts, the contra equity account is reduced by the cost of the shares. Shares released to participants' accounts are charged to compensation expense at their fair market value, not their cost. For earnings-per-share computations, only allocated shares count (i.e., shares that have not been paid off are ignored).

Discontinuing the ESOP. An ESOP might be discontinued for various reasons. For example, the company's employee structure might change or the owners might decide to sell the business to an outsider. The ESOP can be terminated outright, in which case all participants become fully vested. The trustee then liquidates the trust and distributes the assets. Remember that distributions in stock of a closely held company will be subject to the put option requirement mentioned above.

Alternately, the company can simply "freeze" the plan, making no further contributions but continuing the ESOP trust and distributing benefits under the plan's normal schedule as the employees leave. All employees must be fully vested when the plan is frozen.

Finally, the ESOP may be converted into another type of qualified plan, such as a profit-sharing plan.

CHAPTER 14

A Final Caveat

ESOPs are complex, and this book can only give an overview of some main issues. It is *not* intended to provide legal advice or guidance for any particular or individual situation.

The NCEO has many additional resources on ESOPs, including not only a variety of books and seminars available to members and nonmembers alike (although at higher prices for nonmembers) but also the benefits provided to members only: a newsletter, answers to questions, and a referral service (see the following pages for more information). The NCEO's Web site at www.nceo.org includes information on all these resources as well as many articles and news updates on ESOPs, employee stock options, and creating an ownership culture.

To obtain legal advice and set up a plan, you will need to engage the services of experienced ESOP professionals. The members-only area of the NCEO's Web site features the referral service mentioned above (a searchable database of hundreds of employee ownership consultants), as well as advice on how to choose service providers.

Index

ABOUT THE NCEO AND ITS PUBLICATIONS

The National Center for Employee Ownership (NCEO) is a private, non-profit membership and information organization that serves as a central source of information on employee ownership. Supported by its members and services, the NCEO offers a wide range of publications and other resources relating to employee ownership and holds many meetings.

NCEO membership benefits. NCEO members receive:

- The bimonthly newsletter *Employee Ownership Report,* plus the PDF-only newsletter *Equity Compensation Report.*
- Access to the members-only area of the NCEO Web site, including the NCEO's referral service, case studies, and more.
- Substantial discounts on NCEO resources.
- Free live Webinars.
- The right to telephone or email the NCEO for answers to general or specific questions regarding employee ownership.

NCEO membership fees. An introductory NCEO membership costs $90 for one year ($100 outside the U.S.) and covers an entire company at all locations, a single professional offering services in this field, or a single individual with a business interest in employee ownership. Full-time students and faculty members who are not employed in the business sector may join at the academic rate of $40 for one year ($50 outside the U.S.). To join, call us at (510) 208-1300; use the order form on the next page; or sign up online at www.nceo.org.

Other NCEO publications. The NCEO is the world's leading publisher of materials on employee stock plans. This book, *An Introduction to ESOPs,* is $2 for members and $3 for nonmembers. Our full-length books include, among many others, *Understanding ESOPs, S Corporation ESOPs, The ESOP Company Board Handbook,* and *ESOP Valuation,* all of which are $25 for NCEO members and $35 for nonmembers. For ordering information, see the next page. The minimum order is $10. See our Web site at www.nceo.org for a list of all our publications.

ORDER FORM

To order, fill out this form and mail it with your credit card information or check to the NCEO at 1736 Franklin Street, 8th Floor, Oakland, CA 94612; fax it with your credit card information to the NCEO at 510-272-9510; telephone us at 510-208-1300 with your credit card in hand; or order securely online at our Web site, www.nceo.org. If you are not already a member but join now, you will receive the member discount on anything you order.

Name

Organization

Address

City, State, Zip (Country)

Telephone   Fax   Email

Method of Payment: ❑ Check (payable to "NCEO")   ❑ Visa   ❑ M/C   ❑ AMEX

Credit Card Number

Signature   Exp. Date

Checks are accepted only for orders from the U.S. and must be in U.S. currency.

Title	Qty.	Price	Total

Tax: California residents add 8.75% sales tax (on publications only, not membership)

Shipping: In the U.S., $5 for the first book and $1 for each additional one. 10¢ for each booklet (like this), except that there is a minimum shipping charge of $5. Non-U.S. orders are charged actual shipping costs plus $10. No shipping charge for membership.

Introductory NCEO membership: $90 for one year ($100 outside the U.S.)

Subtotal	$
Sales tax	$
Shipping	$
Membership	$
TOTAL DUE	$